THE TEACHER'S TOOL

A Record Keeping Book for Classroom Use

Write Planners and Notebooks

Copyright 2016

All Rights reserved. No part of this book may be reproduced or used in any way or form or by any means whether electronic or mechanical, this means that you cannot record or photocopy any material ideas or tips that are provided in this book.

This record book belongs to

_____

"Education is the key to success in life, and teachers make a lasting impact in the lives of their students.
Solomon Ortiz

today's date _____

time	task

MONTHLY PLANNER

MONDAY				
TUESDAY				
WEDNESDAY				
THURSDAY				
FRIDAY				

today's date _____

schedule

am	6:00	
	7:00	
	8:00	
	9:00	
	10:00	
	11:00	
pm	12:00	
	1:00	
	2:00	
	3:00	
	4:00	
	5:00	
	6:00	
	7:00	

NOTES

today's date _____

time	task

MONTHLY PLANNER

MONDAY				
TUESDAY				
WEDNESDAY				
THURSDAY				
FRIDAY				

today's date _____

schedule

am	6:00
	7:00
	8:00
	9:00
	10:00
	11:00
pm	12:00
	1:00
	2:00
	3:00
	4:00
	5:00
	6:00
	7:00

NOTES

today's date _____

time	task

MONTHLY PLANNER

MONDAY				
TUESDAY				
WEDNESDAY				
THURSDAY				
FRIDAY				

today's date _____

schedule

am	6:00
	7:00
	8:00
	9:00
	10:00
	11:00
pm	12:00
	1:00
	2:00
	3:00
	4:00
	5:00
	6:00
	7:00

NOTES

today's date _____

time	task

MONTHLY PLANNER

MONDAY				
TUESDAY				
WEDNESDAY				
THURSDAY				
FRIDAY				

today's date _____

schedule

am	6:00
	7:00
	8:00
	9:00
	10:00
	11:00
pm	12:00
	1:00
	2:00
	3:00
	4:00
	5:00
	6:00
	7:00

NOTES

today's date _____

time	task

MONTHLY PLANNER

MONDAY				
TUESDAY				
WEDNESDAY				
THURSDAY				
FRIDAY				

today's date _____

schedule

am	6:00	
	7:00	
	8:00	
	9:00	
	10:00	
	11:00	
pm	12:00	
	1:00	
	2:00	
	3:00	
	4:00	
	5:00	
	6:00	
	7:00	

NOTES

today's date _____

time	task

MONTHLY PLANNER

MONDAY				
TUESDAY				
WEDNESDAY				
THURSDAY				
FRIDAY				

today's date _____

schedule

am	6:00	
	7:00	
	8:00	
	9:00	
	10:00	
	11:00	
pm	12:00	
	1:00	
	2:00	
	3:00	
	4:00	
	5:00	
	6:00	
	7:00	

NOTES

today's date _____

time	task

MONTHLY PLANNER

MONDAY				
TUESDAY				
WEDNESDAY				
THURSDAY				
FRIDAY				

today's date _____

schedule

am	6:00	
	7:00	
	8:00	
	9:00	
	10:00	
	11:00	
pm	12:00	
	1:00	
	2:00	
	3:00	
	4:00	
	5:00	
	6:00	
	7:00	

NOTES

today's date _____

time	task

MONTHLY PLANNER

MONDAY				
TUESDAY				
WEDNESDAY				
THURSDAY				
FRIDAY				

today's date _____

schedule

am	6:00	
	7:00	
	8:00	
	9:00	
	10:00	
	11:00	
pm	12:00	
	1:00	
	2:00	
	3:00	
	4:00	
	5:00	
	6:00	
	7:00	

NOTES

today's date ———————

time	task

MONTHLY PLANNER

MONDAY				
TUESDAY				
WEDNESDAY				
THURSDAY				
FRIDAY				

today's date _____

schedule

am	6:00
	7:00
	8:00
	9:00
	10:00
	11:00
pm	12:00
	1:00
	2:00
	3:00
	4:00
	5:00
	6:00
	7:00

NOTES

today's date _____

time	task

MONTHLY PLANNER

MONDAY				
TUESDAY				
WEDNESDAY				
THURSDAY				
FRIDAY				

today's date _____

schedule

am	6:00
	7:00
	8:00
	9:00
	10:00
	11:00
pm	12:00
	1:00
	2:00
	3:00
	4:00
	5:00
	6:00
	7:00

NOTES

today's date _____

time	task

MONTHLY PLANNER

MONDAY				
TUESDAY				
WEDNESDAY				
THURSDAY				
FRIDAY				

today's date _____

schedule

am	6:00
	7:00
	8:00
	9:00
	10:00
	11:00
pm	12:00
	1:00
	2:00
	3:00
	4:00
	5:00
	6:00
	7:00

NOTES

today's date _____

time	task

MONTHLY PLANNER

MONDAY				
TUESDAY				
WEDNESDAY				
THURSDAY				
FRIDAY				

today's date _____

schedule

am	6:00	
	7:00	
	8:00	
	9:00	
	10:00	
	11:00	
pm	12:00	
	1:00	
	2:00	
	3:00	
	4:00	
	5:00	
	6:00	
	7:00	

NOTES

today's date _____

time	task

MONTHLY PLANNER

MONDAY			
TUESDAY			
WEDNESDAY			
THURSDAY			
FRIDAY			

today's date _____

schedule

am	6:00	
	7:00	
	8:00	
	9:00	
	10:00	
	11:00	
pm	12:00	
	1:00	
	2:00	
	3:00	
	4:00	
	5:00	
	6:00	
	7:00	

NOTES

today's date _____

time	task

MONTHLY PLANNER

MONDAY				
TUESDAY				
WEDNESDAY				
THURSDAY				
FRIDAY				

today's date _____

schedule	
am	6:00
	7:00
	8:00
	9:00
	10:00
	11:00
pm	12:00
	1:00
	2:00
	3:00
	4:00
	5:00
	6:00
	7:00

NOTES

today's date _____

time	task

MONTHLY PLANNER

MONDAY				
TUESDAY				
WEDNESDAY				
THURSDAY				
FRIDAY				

today's date _____

schedule

am	6:00	
	7:00	
	8:00	
	9:00	
	10:00	
	11:00	
pm	12:00	
	1:00	
	2:00	
	3:00	
	4:00	
	5:00	
	6:00	
	7:00	

NOTES

today's date _____

time	task

MONTHLY PLANNER

MONDAY				
TUESDAY				
WEDNESDAY				
THURSDAY				
FRIDAY				

today's date _____

schedule

am	6:00
	7:00
	8:00
	9:00
	10:00
	11:00
pm	12:00
	1:00
	2:00
	3:00
	4:00
	5:00
	6:00
	7:00

NOTES

today's date _____

time	task

MONTHLY PLANNER

MONDAY				
TUESDAY				
WEDNESDAY				
THURSDAY				
FRIDAY				

today's date _____

schedule

am	6:00
	7:00
	8:00
	9:00
	10:00
	11:00
pm	12:00
	1:00
	2:00
	3:00
	4:00
	5:00
	6:00
	7:00

NOTES

today's date _____

time	task

MONTHLY PLANNER

MONDAY				
TUESDAY				
WEDNESDAY				
THURSDAY				
FRIDAY				

today's date _____

schedule

am	6:00	
	7:00	
	8:00	
	9:00	
	10:00	
	11:00	
pm	12:00	
	1:00	
	2:00	
	3:00	
	4:00	
	5:00	
	6:00	
	7:00	

NOTES

today's date _____

time	task

MONTHLY PLANNER

MONDAY				
TUESDAY				
WEDNESDAY				
THURSDAY				
FRIDAY				

today's date _____

schedule

am	6:00	
	7:00	
	8:00	
	9:00	
	10:00	
	11:00	
pm	12:00	
	1:00	
	2:00	
	3:00	
	4:00	
	5:00	
	6:00	
	7:00	

NOTES

today's date _____

time	task

MONTHLY PLANNER

MONDAY				
TUESDAY				
WEDNESDAY				
THURSDAY				
FRIDAY				

today's date _____

schedule

am	6:00	
	7:00	
	8:00	
	9:00	
	10:00	
	11:00	
pm	12:00	
	1:00	
	2:00	
	3:00	
	4:00	
	5:00	
	6:00	
	7:00	

NOTES

today's date _____

time	task

MONTHLY PLANNER

MONDAY				
TUESDAY				
WEDNESDAY				
THURSDAY				
FRIDAY				

today's date _____

schedule

am	6:00	
	7:00	
	8:00	
	9:00	
	10:00	
	11:00	
pm	12:00	
	1:00	
	2:00	
	3:00	
	4:00	
	5:00	
	6:00	
	7:00	

NOTES

today's date _____

time	task

MONTHLY PLANNER

MONDAY			
TUESDAY			
WEDNESDAY			
THURSDAY			
FRIDAY			

today's date _____

schedule

am	6:00	
	7:00	
	8:00	
	9:00	
	10:00	
	11:00	
pm	12:00	
	1:00	
	2:00	
	3:00	
	4:00	
	5:00	
	6:00	
	7:00	

NOTES

today's date _____

time	task

MONTHLY PLANNER

MONDAY				
TUESDAY				
WEDNESDAY				
THURSDAY				
FRIDAY				

today's date _____

		schedule
am	6:00	
	7:00	
	8:00	
	9:00	
	10:00	
	11:00	
pm	12:00	
	1:00	
	2:00	
	3:00	
	4:00	
	5:00	
	6:00	
	7:00	

NOTES

today's date _____

time	task

MONTHLY PLANNER

MONDAY				
TUESDAY				
WEDNESDAY				
THURSDAY				
FRIDAY				

today's date _____

schedule

am	6:00
	7:00
	8:00
	9:00
	10:00
	11:00
pm	12:00
	1:00
	2:00
	3:00
	4:00
	5:00
	6:00
	7:00

NOTES

today's date _____

time	task

MONTHLY PLANNER

MONDAY				
TUESDAY				
WEDNESDAY				
THURSDAY				
FRIDAY				

NOTES

www.ingramcontent.com/pod-product-compliance
Lightning Source LLC
Chambersburg PA
CBHW081016040426
42444CB00014B/3229